english sign language

READING COMPREHENSION ACTIVITIES

M. R. Pearce

Harrap London

First published in Great Britain 1977
by GEORGE G. HARRAP & CO. LTD.
182-184 High Holborn, London WC1V 7AX

© *M. R. Pearce 1977*

ISBN 0 245 53127 0

Set by Harry Darton & Associates Ltd
Printed in Great Britain by David Green
(Printers) Ltd, Kettering, Northamptonshire

PREFACE

The purpose of this book is to expose students of English to the kind of reading matter which would inevitably face them in England, but which tends to be neglected in schools. The student may not need to read books or newspapers, and yet it seems to be taken for granted that everyone can read and understand the multitude of notices and signs in the streets, in shops, and on all forms of packaging. Failure to understand this 'sign language' may lead to inconvenience, embarrassment, expense, even danger.

Some 120 photographs of actual signs and notices are provided. It is hoped that, by studying them, understanding them, and making use of the language they contain in imaginary related situations, the student will acquire not only some very practical language and skill, but also some familiarity with England, the English and their way of life.

The photographs cover thirteen topics or themes seen as being of immediate importance: entering and leaving Britain; travel by train, bus and car; food and drink; accommodation; towns; shops; countryside; places of interest; seaside; communications; leisure; danger; medical.

Although the photographs were almost all taken in the North of England—in York, on Tyneside, in the Lake District National Park, and in localities visited on the way to and from these areas—similar signs can be seen all over England.

M.R.P.

CONTENTS

Entering and Leaving Britain   7

Travel: Trains   12

Travel: Buses   15

Travel: Cars   17

Food and Drink   23

Accommodation   29

Town   33

Shops   38

Country   43

Places of Interest   47

Seaside   51

Communications   55

Leisure   58

Danger   62

Medical   66

TEACHER'S NOTES

Arrangement

The photographs are grouped according to thirteen themes. Some themes receive greater emphasis than others. This reflects their importance (particularly for the visitor), the amount and variety of reading that is likely to be encountered in everyday life and the degree of difficulty likely to be experienced in the actual situation.

Within each theme the material is roughly graded according to the degree of difficulty. This is related mainly to the amount and complexity of the language to be sifted by the reader in order to solve the problem posed by each sign.

Preparation

The teacher will no doubt wish to prepare a lesson on 'sign language' — particularly with less advanced students — by making sure that they have (a) acquired the necessary vocabulary, (b) at least some understanding of the situation of the signs in question, and (c) that they are familiar with the language structures demanded by the exploitation. To this end, a brief explanation of the situation accompanies each photograph. There are also notes(•) on unusual or difficult words or usage, and background information where necessary.

Exploitation

It is intended that the photographs should be exploited at different levels, and that the teacher should decide the level appropriate for his or her students. Indeed, the teacher may find it useful to work through different levels, requiring increasingly demanding responses from students.

Three kinds of exploitation are suggested.

A. Simple questions designed to test comprehension. The questions may be answered orally or in writing, in English or the mother tongue, at the teacher's discretion. This is the simplest level of exploitation and should be within the grasp of students who have reached the intermediate level, provided that they are adequately prepared. It is important that both students and teachers should understand that there is not always a clear-cut answer to the questions. It may be correct to answer that you cannot know for certain, or it may be that there is more than one correct answer. This is often the case in real life.

B. The second level of exploitation requires students to ask questions, or initiate a conversation, in English in order to solve a problem, or to respond to a situation related to the sign in question. Clearly the teacher may make varying demands upon the students. Quite simple sentences could be acceptable in the case of less advanced students. The work is intended to be oral.

Exploitation material of types A and B normally accompanies each photograph. The third type has been included less often, but the following general suggestions are offered for teachers who would like to extend this level of exploitation.

C. The third level consists of rôle-playing activities as an extension of B. In this case two people are involved: the students in pairs or a student and the teacher. The first student plays the part of a foreign visitor to England and the second student or the teacher plays the part of the native English speaker. More or less complex and demanding exchanges of questions and answers can be developed as the two characters play out their rôles. The student should be placed in a situation as near realistic as possible.

Follow-up

Follow-up activities might take the form of written work such as dialogues or narratives related to the exploitation already carried out. Alternately, some teachers might like to set work requiring students to do individual research on topics associated with the themes and signs. A comparative approach can be especially worthwhile, in which students consciously compare and contrast customs, laws, attitudes or practices in England with those of their own country.

It is not, however, the intention to determine the methods of any teacher, but to offer material which may be adapted to their own particular methods and requirements.

entering and leaving britain

Belgique/Belgie France
BR Deutschland Italia
Danmark Luxembourg
Nederland Irish Republic

EEC

passports

1 You have just arrived in Britain by air,
and you see these signs in the airport buildings.

•The initials EEC stand for European
Economic Community, also called the Common Market.

A.1 What are the people in the queue waiting for?

.2 Would you go to one of these
positions if you were
a) Dutch?   d) Swedish?
b) German?   e) American?
c) British?   f) Japanese?

2

A.1 The people in the photograph are
going up the escalators for two
reasons. What are they?

B. You have waited to reclaim your
cases but have not been able to find
them on the conveyor belt. What do
you say to the porter?

↑ Baggage
reclaim
belt
numbers 1,2,3,4   ↑ Customs —

DUTY-FREE ALLOWANCES

If you have come from an EEC country (see list below) the allowances in column 1 apply to goods obtained duty and tax-paid within the EEC. The allowances in column 2 apply if any of the goods were obtained outside the EEC or in a duty and tax-free shop, or duty and tax-free on a ship or aircraft.

If you have come from a country outside the EEC the allowances in column 2 apply.

	1	**2**	
Tobacco Goods			
Cigarettes	300	200	
or			
Cigarillos	150	100	double if you live outside Europe
or			
Cigars	75	50	
or			
Tobacco	400 grammes	250 grammes	
Alcoholic Drinks			
over 38·8° proof (22° Gay-Lussac)	1½ litres	1 litre	
or			
not over 38·8° proof *or* fortified *or* sparkling wine	3 litres	2 litres	
plus			
still table wine	3 litres	2 litres	
Persons under 17 are not entitled to tobacco and drinks allowances			
Perfume	75 grammes (3 fl. oz. or 90 cc)	50 grammes (2 fl. oz. or 60 cc)	
Toilet water	375 cc (13 fl. oz.)	250 cc (9 fl. oz.)	
Other goods	£50 worth	£10 worth	

and, **if you are visiting the United Kingdom for less than 6 months,** all personal effects (except tobacco goods, wine, spirits and perfume) which you intend to take with you when you leave.

The countries of the EEC are Belgium, Denmark, France, West Germany, the Irish Republic, Italy, Luxembourg, the Netherlands and the United Kingdom. (The Channel Islands are treated as outside the EEC.)

3 This list shows what you are allowed to bring into Britain without having to pay customs duty.

A.1 How many cigarettes bought in West Germany are you allowed?

2 How many cigarettes bought in Austria are you allowed?

3 You have brought 75 cc. of perfume in Spain. Will you have to pay any duty on it?

4 If you are 15 years old how many cigarettes are you allowed to bring into Britain from Italy?

5 You have bought some table wine in a duty-free shop on a ferry. How much are you allowed to bring into Britain without paying duty?

6 The symbol '£' is an abbreviation. For which word? What does it mean?

B. You have bought some presents for the British friends you are going to visit and you are not sure if the place where you bought them is an EEC country or not. What do you say to the customs officer?

4 This photograph shows customs officers inspecting luggage, and two special signs which are sometimes used to show travellers which way to go through the customs hall.

A.1 You are coming to Britain for a short holiday. Which sign do you follow if you have got
   a) 500 cigarettes?
   b) a bottle of ordinary wine?
   c) a dog?
   d) your new ciné camera worth £75.00?

C. You are in the customs hall. You walk through the 'Nothing to declare' section. A customs officer stops you and asks if you have anything to declare. You say that you have not. The officer asks you to open one of your cases. When you do so he finds a small bottle of brandy. You explain that you had forgotten about it, and that you bought it as a gift. Reconstruct the conversation, including the customs officer's questions.

GOODS to declare

NOTHING to declare

5

A. You see this sign in an airport terminal.
Would you go through these doors
   a) to meet a person arriving by plane?
   b) to catch a bus to the city?
   c) to have a meal before your flight?
   d) to make a telephone call?
   e) to collect your luggage after arrival?

B. You have arrived at the airport and
want a taxi to take you to the city.
The sign tells you nothing about
taxis, so you ask an official where to
go to find one. What do you say?

6

Before you leave Britain you go to the duty-free shop in the airport terminal building.

A.1 What sort of things can you buy in the duty-free shop?

2 If you were in the duty-free shop how would you know if the time of your flight had been changed?

3 The sign in the duty-free shop directs you downstairs to Gates 30-39 and Gates 10-19. Are these 'Gates'
   a) access points to planes?
   b) duty-free shop checkouts?
   c) exits from the airport building?
   d) customs barriers?
   e) passport control points?

B. You go to the duty-free shop to buy a present. You find just what you want, but have not enough money to pay for it. Explain your problem and ask if you can use a travellers' cheque.

7 One of the first things you see on arrival at one port of entry is this sign at the entrance to a fenced area.

    A.1 Which travellers must follow the direction of the arrow?

      2 Why?

    B. You have nothing to declare. Ask the official on duty if you must still follow the arrow.

8 This poster is in the window of the cabin seen in the previous photograph.

    A.1 What is 'rabies'?

      2 Why is rabies so dangerous?

      3 How could rabies enter Britain?

      4 Who can catch rabies?

      5 What are the penalties for smuggling animals into Britain?

    C. Imagine that you are coming to Britain for at least a year and you bring your pet cat with you in your car. The customs officer explains that your cat must stay in quarantine. You ask how long for and how much it will cost. The customs officer says that the quarantine period is six months, but he does not know what the cost will be. Reconstruct the conversation.

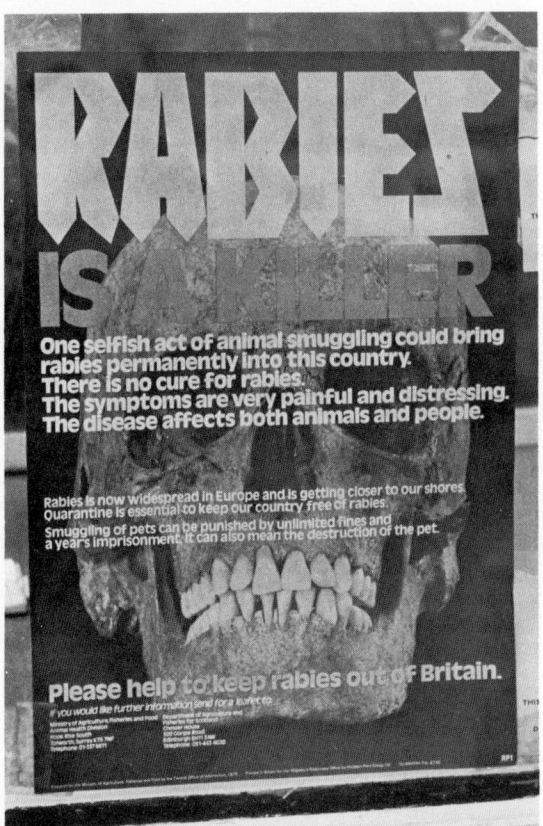

9 You are leaving the docks at one of the ports of entry and you see this sign beside the road.
• **This sign is outside Newcastle at the main port of entry to Britain, by sea, from Norway.**

A.1 Who in particular should read this sign?

2 What exactly does it tell you to do?

3 Why is the sign necessary?

10 This sign is at a road junction in the centre of a city.

A.1 How far is it to the airport?

2 You are at the junction. Would you expect to see a car approaching from your right?

3 Would you go to the motorail terminal if you wanted
a) to travel by train with your car?
b) to send your car by train in advance?
c) to travel by train and leave your car in a special car park?
d) to return a hired car to the railway station?

B. You cannot find the motorail terminal and decide to ask your way. What do you say?

travel: trains

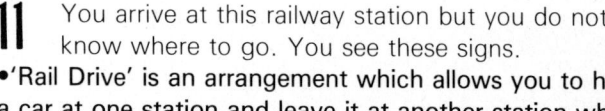

11 You arrive at this railway station but you do not know where to go. You see these signs.

• 'Rail Drive' is an arrangement which allows you to hire a car at one station and leave it at another station while you continue your journey by train.

• Day Return tickets, which can be used only on the same day, are sold at less than normal prices.

• Children up to 14 years old pay half of the normal fare.

A. Which sign should you follow
   a) to find out the times of trains to London?
   b) to book a seat on a train for the following day?
   c) to arrange for a hired car to meet you in Edinburgh?
   d) to book a sleeper on the night train to London?
   e) to buy a second-class return ticket to Manchester?
   f) to board the train for York?
   g) to get a cheap day return ticket to Carlisle?

B. You wish to travel to London tomorrow afternoon with two friends and your ten year old sister. Ask for the tickets you need, and for the times of trains to London.

12 This ticket machine is at a railway station.

• You are not allowed to go through the barriers at the entrance to the platform unless you have either a train ticket or a platform ticket.

A.1 Why would you want to buy a ticket?
  2 How much does a ticket cost?
  3 What does 'p' mean?

B. You wish to buy a ticket from the machine but you only have a 50p coin. You ask someone for change. What do you say?

eparturcs

Platform	Platform	Platform
11	**9**	**10**
16-30	15.51	1545
Blaydon	Darlington	Darlington
Wylam	York	York
Prudhoe	Doncaster	Doncaster
Stocksfield		London
Riding Mill	Peterborough	King's Cross
Corbridge	London	
Hexham		

13 This board is at a large railway station.

A.1 Does the board tell you when trains arrive or leave?

2 When does the train for Peterborough leave the station?

3 Which platform should you go to if you want the train for Darlington?

B.1 You are taking a train to Edinburgh. Ask at the information desk which platform the train leaves from and what time it leaves.

2 You are meeting a friend who is coming from London. Ask what time the train will arrive and if it might be late.

uggage lockers

Fee for 24 hours' use

Large	20p
Medium	20p
Small	15p

Articles deposited will be removed after 24 hours to the Left luggage office

Hours of Business

Monday to Saturday 06.30 to 22.00
Sunday 09.00 to 22.00

14 This notice is near the luggage lockers at a railway station.

A.1 What is a 'locker'?

2 When would you use a luggage locker?

3 How long can you leave your luggage in a locker?

4 How much will it cost to deposit a brief-case?

5 Where will your luggage be taken if you leave it in the locker for more than 24 hours?

B. You deposit your brief-case at 9.30 p.m. on Friday and come to collect it at 8.30 a.m. on Sunday. The locker is empty so you find a railway official at the left luggage office. What do you say to claim your brief-case? You will need to describe it.

Take a bargain day trip from Morecambe

Bentham	84p*	Grange-O-Sands	97p*
Carnforth	56p	Lancaster	40p
Clapham	97p*	Skipton	£1·70
Giggleswick	£1·00*	Windermere	£1·40*

*Mondays to Fridays only and no half fares

Ask at station for details

15 This advertisement is at Morecambe railway station and shows special cheap day fares to certain places. You would like to go to Windermere with your friend and her ten year old brother.

   A.1 When can you take a bargain day trip to Windermere?
      2 Do children pay less?

3 What does the sign tell you to do if you want more information?

B. You go inside the station to ask for more information. Ask about the times of trains to and from Windermere, and how long the journey takes. Then ask for tickets for the day of your choice.

16 This is the window of a travel agency.
•'Senior Citizens' are retired people and are also known as old age pensioners (*see* •101).

   A.1 Is it possible to book a seat on a train here?
      2 Can you obtain information here about air fares to Frankfurt?
      3 Can you buy Swiss francs?
      4 Can you arrange a holiday for your grandmother here?

5 Can you buy railway tickets to Rome?
6 Can you book a sea passage from Britain to the U.S.A.?

B. You are on holiday and have to return home as quickly as possible. You go to this travel agency to obtain all the necessary information for the journey to your home town. What questions must you ask?

travel:buses

17 This bus stop is in a street in York.
- At some bus stops in England—'Request stops'—you have to signal to the driver if you want the bus to stop.

  A.1 Where should you stand if you are waiting for the bus to Leeds?

  2 Which bus goes to Dringhouses?

  3 Do you have to signal to the driver if you wish the bus to stop, or will buses always stop here?

  B. You wish to go by bus to Tadcaster, which is between York and Leeds, but you do not know if this is the right stop or how often the buses run. Ask another person waiting at the stop.

18 This bus is about to leave the bus station just as you arrive. You are in a great hurry.
- Remember that in Britain vehicles keep to the left, so the doors of a bus are on the left-hand side.

  A.1 What does 'No Entry' mean?

  2 Would you go right or left to reach the front of the bus?

  B. You get on the bus, but you are not sure if it is the right bus to take you to Ashington. What do you say to the driver?

19 This poster advertises the 'Park and Ride' scheme, which encourages shoppers to leave their cars outside the town centre.

A.1 What does 'Park and Ride' mean?

  2 When can you use the scheme?

  3 Where do motorists park when they use this scheme?

  4 Does it cost anything to park under this scheme?

B. You are driving into town when you see this poster. You stop the car and ask a passer-by how to use the scheme. What do you say?

travel:cars

20 You are travelling along the A1 when you come to these signs.
•Roads are classified by using the letters M for motorways, A for main roads and B for secondary roads. Minor roads are not numbered.
•(M) means that, although the road is not a motorway, motorway rules apply to it.

A.1 What type of road is the A1 here?

2 Should you go straight on or turn left here if you are:
a) a hitch-hiker hoping for a lift?
b) going to Jesmond?
c) an experienced car driver?
d) riding a bicycle?

B. You are in a car travelling towards the centre of the city where you wish to do some shopping. You reach this road junction and stop. You want to know which road you should take to find a parking place. What do you say when you ask a passer-by?

21 You are driving with an English friend along this road and you pass this sign. You are travelling fast.

A.1 What ought your friend to do on seeing the sign?

2 Why ought he to do this?

B. You realize that your friend has not seen the sign. What do you say to him when you pass the sign?

22 This sign is just outside the village of Grasmere in the Lake District, an area which is very popular with walkers.

  A.1 You wish to drive to the village of Chapel Stile in the next valley. Does this sign mean that you cannot drive to the village along this road?

    2 The walker is also going to Chapel Stile. Should she take this road?

  B. You are not sure if you can drive to Chapel Stile this way. Ask the walker if she is going to Chapel Stile and if you can get there by car on this road.

23 You are driving through a large park and you see this notice as you approach the exit.

  A.1 What *two* things does the sign tell you to do?

    2 Are the gates to the park open all day?

  B. An English friend is driving you in his car through the park towards this gateway. You see that it is half past four in the afternoon. What do you tell your friend?

24

This is an 'Urban Clearway' sign.

• A 'clearway' is a road kept clear of parked vehicles at certain times in order to allow a free-flow of traffic.

A.1 Would you find this sign in the country?

2 What does the word 'clearway' mean to the motorist?

3 On what days is stopping restricted?

4 At what times is stopping restricted?

C. You are visiting a friend who lives in this road and you have parked the car outside the house at the side of the road. You ask your friend if you are allowed to park here. He explains when you may and may not park. Reconstruct the conversation.

25

Double or single yellow lines along the edge of the road mean that parking is restricted. The exact restrictions are usually shown on small signs fixed to posts.

A.1 When are you allowed to park here?

2 Can you wait here to pick up a passenger or parcel
   a) at half past eight in the morning?
   b) at five o'clock in the afternoon?
   c) at midday?
   d) at seven-thirty in the morning?

B. You are driving through a town. Your friend asks if you can stop because he wants to take a photograph of a church not far away. You do not notice the double yellow lines along the edge of the road. After two or three minutes a policeman tells you that you are not allowed to park there. What do you say?

COMPUTER CONTROLLED CAR PARK

PAY AT EXIT
BY COIN MACHINES

5p - 10p - 50p COINS ONLY

PLEASE HAVE THESE
COINS AVAILABLE

26 This board is in a modern multi-storey car park.

A.1 Does the sign tell you to pay as you leave the car park?

2 Can you pay with a pound note?

3 Where do you put the money when you pay?

B. At the exit from the car park you find that you do not have the right coins to operate the machine. What do you say to the attendant to explain your problem?

HOW TO
DRIVE OUT

put 10° in slot
and barrier will
rise automatically

EMERGENCY

in case of failure
of mechanism or
accident phone

Hexham 401
Hexham 4 11

27 You are leaving a car park in Hexham and find that the barrier at the exit is down.

A.1 How much does it cost to park here?

2 What must you do to make the barrier lift?

3 What does the sign tell you to do if the barrier does not lift?

B. You follow the instructions but the barrier does not lift, so you follow the further instructions. What do you say to the person who answers the telephone?

28 This is a parking meter in a city centre.
•Parking meters are found in the centre of most large towns. You may expect to pay 5p or 10p to park your car for a limited length of time.

A.1 How many cars can use this meter?
  2 How long may you park at this meter?
  3 How much does it cost?
  4 What coins must you use in the meter?
  5 When is parking free at this meter?
B. You wish to park at this meter but do not have the correct coin. Ask a passer-by if she can change a 50p piece for you and explain why you need a 2p piece in the change.

29 This car park is in a small town in the Lake District.

A.1 Are you allowed to park a caravan here?
  2 How much does it cost to park your car here all night?
  3 Are you allowed to sleep in your car in this car park?
C. Reconstruct the following conversation. You are intending to sleep in the car park in your caravan, but the attendant tells you that it is not permitted. You ask where you must go and he tells you about camp sites not far away. You ask where the closest one is and he tells you it is near the lake. But you do not know where the lake is and it is now dark. The attendant tells you the way.

30 This sign is outside a garage in a small village.

•The forecourt is the area in front of the garage where the petrol pumps are.

•The times at which petrol may be bought vary widely: some filling stations are open 24 hours a day; others are open during normal shop hours only (9.00 a.m.-5.30 p.m.).

A.1 Is the garage open at 8.30 in the evening?

2 If not, where can you get petrol from?

C. It is seven o'clock on Sunday morning and you need petrol. Ask another motorist how you can get petrol. What does he say in reply?

31 These instructions are displayed at a garage. They tell customers how to operate the self-service pumps.

•The grades of petrol are usually indicated by the number of stars—2, 3, 4 or 5. More stars mean more expensive petrol. 'Super' is usually 4-star petrol.

A.1 The pumps deliver three different grades of petrol. How do you obtain the grade for your car?

2 What must you do to start the petrol flowing?

3 When will the petrol stop flowing?

4 What are you reminded to do after filling your tank?

5 Put the instructions of the sign into spoken English. For example—1. Choose the kind of petrol you want.

food and drink

32 This sign is near a restaurant.
- A.1 What is the name of the restaurant?
- 2 Does the restaurant offer waitress service?
- 3 Can you get a meal at this restaurant now?
- B. You wish to have a meal before catching a bus in only 30 minutes time and there is a long queue outside the restaurant. Ask a passer-by to direct you to another suitable restaurant, and explain why you are in a hurry.

33 This sign is at the entrance to a small country hotel.
- A.1 What sort of meal is being advertised?
- 2 When could you get this kind of meal? (*See* photograph 34 for a little help.)
- 3 Does the sign tell you if you can get a bar lunch now?
- B. You enter the hotel to ask about the bar lunches. What do you say to the barman?

BRANDLING ARMS

GRILL ROOM

OPENING HOURS
MONDAY to SATURDAY
12 NOON - 2 P.M.

PHONE - 856718

34 This sign is outside a pub called the Brandling Arms.

•Public houses (pubs) are not open all the time. There are 'licenced hours' during which drinks may be sold. The hours vary from area to area, but a typical pub might be open for the sale of drinks from 11.00 a.m. to 3.00 p.m. and from 6.00 p.m. to 10.30 p.m. They may provide non-alcoholic drinks at other times.

A.1 What kind of food is available in a grill room?

2 Is the grill room open for the same periods as the public house?

3 When is the grill room closed?

B. You telephone the Brandling Arms to find out about their meals. Ask about the times and prices and whether it is necessary to book a table.

Menu

FRIED FISH & CHIPS

SAUSAGE, EGG & CHIPS

STEAK PIE & CHIPS

COLD MEAT with SALAD or CHIPS

INCLUDING POT of TEA
BREAD & BUTTER

95P

VAT INCLUSIVE

35 This menu is by the door of a seaside café. You and two friends decide to go in for a meal.

•V.A.T. stands for Value Added Tax. (*See* also •40.)

A.1 One friend does not like meat. Which meal must she choose?

2 Another friend does not like potatoes. Which meal must he choose?

3 What must you choose if you do not want a hot meal?

4 What drink is served with the meal?

5 Will V.A.T. be added to the price of the meal?

6 What will the total bill be for the three of you? How much change will you get from a £5 note?

B. You are in the café with your friends. Tell the waitress that you are ready to order and order for all three of you.

36 Dale Lodge is a hotel in Grasmere in the Lake District.

•The licensing laws forbid anyone under the age of 18 to buy or drink alcohol in a pub, hotel or any other public place.

•Afternoon tea normally consists of tea, bread and butter (or toast) and cakes. 'High tea', which is not common in the South of England, is a much larger, hot meal normally eaten in the late afternoon or early evening.

A.1 What meals are available here?

2 What meal would you order if you were very hungry at 5.30 p.m.?

3 What are 'minerals'?

4 What kinds of drink are available in the café?

5 Can you buy alcoholic drinks in the café?

B. You arrive at Dale Lodge at 2.30 p.m. Ask the waitress in the café if lunch is still being served.

37 This board stands on the pavement outside the Cellar Bar.

A.1 Would you go up or down the steps if you were looking for this bar?

2 Can you get anything other than drinks at the bar?

3 Which of the following would you expect to be able to buy here: tea, coffee, cold milk, sherry, whisky, Carlsberg, Martini, Coca-cola, brandy?

4 What does it cost to have a party in a room here?

5 If you did not have very much money, would you go into the Cellar Bar for something to eat?

B. You would like to eat here at 7.30 p.m. but you have only got 30p. Ask the barman if you can buy a meal for this amount and if there is a menu.

38 You are looking for somewhere to have a meal when you see these signs.

A.1 There are three different places where you can get something to eat advertised here. What are they?

2 Which of the three places would you go to if you wanted:
   a) sausage, egg and chips, with a cup of coffee?
   b) a glass of wine or beer in the evening?
   c) dinner at eight o'clock each evening for a week?
   d) a sandwich, a bar of chocolate and a coke?
   e) poached egg on toast for breakfast?

3 Can you eat at the Dale Lodge Hotel if you are not staying there?

39 This restaurant specializes in meals of a particular sort.

A.1 Which of the following would you be able to obtain here:
   a) egg and bacon
   b) plaice and chips
   c) mussels
   d) a glass of beer
   e) a chateaubriand
   f) fresh salmon
   g) scampi
   h) shrimps?

2 What does 'Est. 1880' mean?

C. In this restaurant you order plaice and chips, but when the waitress brings them you find that they are cold. You complain and ask the waitress to take them back. She does so but tells you that the cooks have finished and that you will have to have something cold. You order salmon and salad, which is much more expensive. You are angry and say so. Reconstruct the conversation.

40 This poster shows the prices of cooked dishes available in a small shop and café.

• There are many 'take-away' shops like this one, as V.A.T. is not charged on food which is taken away and eaten elsewhere, but must be paid on food eaten in a restaurant.

A.1 Would you pay the same prices if you eat your meal in the café?

2 What does the abbreviation 'qtr.' mean?

3 What could you afford to eat and drink if you had 50p?

4 Can you buy any drinks other than coffee and Pepsi Cola?

5 If you do not like chips what could you have instead of them?

B. You and your two friends want something to eat and drink. You have £2.00 between you. One of your friends does not like chicken. Decide what you will buy and add up the cost. Go into the shop and order what you want.

41 This menu is displayed outside a pub.

• A 'Ploughman's' (lunch) is a cold snack usually consisting of bread, butter, lettuce, tomato and cheese, and is often available in pubs.

A.1 When can you get a meal here?

2 What could you get to eat when meals are not available?

3 What cold meal could you buy?

4 If you do not eat meat what could you have?

5 What would you have if you liked oriental dishes?

B. You have ordered a meat dish by mistake. Ask the barman if you can change your order and have an omelette instead.

Take-Out Trade

WHOLE CHICKEN	1·30p
HALF "	75p
HALF CHICKEN with CHIPS	88p
QTR. "	40p
QTR. " with CHIPS	53p
HOT PIE & CHIPS	31p
SAUSAGE & CHIPS	29p
HOT PIES	17p
PEPSI COLA etc.	14p
COFFEE	8p
CHIPS BAG	13p
BREAD ROLLS 4p • GIBLETS	14p

A SELECTION OF THE FOLLOWING HOT AND COLD DISHES AVAILABLE MON TO FRI 12 NOON TO 2 P.M.

Soup from the Pot	15
Chunky Sausages, Onion Sauce, Peas, Potatoes	45
Gammon and Eggs Platter	110
Sue's Home-Made Steak Pie	60
Madras Curry and Rice	60
Coach and Horses Lamb Platter	100
Shepherds Pie and Pickles	40
Deep Fried Haddock, Chips and Peas	60
Grilled Steak Platter	120
Omelettes **from 40p**	
Special Soup and Sandwich Platter	50
Ploughmans Lunch	35
Fruit Pie and Cream	20
Chocolate Paris Sundae	20
Cheese and Biscuits	20
Coffee	12

Sandwiches Always Available

CE CAFETERIA PRICES

TEA	7p	FRIED EGG & CHIPS	35p
COFFEE	12p	PORK SAUSAGE & CHIPS	45p
MILK	8p	HOT DOG	15p
FRIED HADDOCK & CHIPS	40p	EGG SALAD	45p
MEAT & POTATO PIE & PEAS	50p	CHEESE "	45p
STEAK & KIDNEY PIE & CHIPS	42p	HAM "	55p
MEAT PIE & CHIPS	40p	ROAST BEEF "	55p
BEANS & CHIPS	30p	CHICKEN "	60p
HAMBURGER	24p	BUTTER	6p
PEAS	9p	BOILED HAM SANDWICH	22p
FRUIT COCKTAIL	18p	ROAST BEEF "	22p
" " WITH FRESH CREAM	25p	CHEESE "	18p

42 These prices are displayed on a large board outside a self-service cafeteria.

A.1 How many hot dishes are available?

2 What cold meals are available?

3 What kinds of sandwiches are on sale?

4 What could you have if you wanted a cold drink?

5 What could you have if you were a vegetarian?

B. You have gone into the cafeteria and you are serving yourself from the shelves. You would like a ham salad but there are none left. What do you say to the assistant?

43 This price list is displayed in the window of another café.

•'Horlicks' is the brand name of a malt-flavoured powder which is mixed with milk as a drink.

A.1 What drinks are on sale?

2 How much will a sandwich cost?

3 What sweet dishes are available?

4 Can you get a milk drink here?

5 Is there any soup available?

6 How is the egg cooked when you have egg and chips?

B. In this café you order egg and chips. The waitress brings you meat pie and chips. What do you say to the waitress?

SIRLOIN STEAK & CHIPS	99	MEAT PIE & CHIPS	42	FRUIT SUNDAE	25
CHICKEN & CHIPS	70	BACON SANDWICH	35	MILK SHAKES	15
BACON & CHIPS	55	APPLE PIE & CREAM	25	HOT CHOCOLATE	15
HAMBURGER & CHIPS	48	HOT DOGS	18	HORLICKS	15
STEAK PUDDING & CHIPS	45	HAMBURGER	22	MINERALS	10
STEAK & KIDNEY PIE & CHIPS	45	SANDWICHES from	18	COFFEE	12
FISH & CHIPS	46	PORTION OF PEAS	10	MILK	10
EGG & CHIPS	36	CAKES from	8	TEA	8
PORK SAUSAGES & CHIPS	42	BREAD & BUTTER	7		

accommodation

44 You are driving along a country road looking for a camp site. You see this board at the top of a grassy lane.

A.1 Have you:
- a) passed the site?
- b) arrived at the site?
- c) some distance to go to reach the site?

2 Does the sign tell you if caravans or motor caravans are allowed on this site?

B. You arrive at the site in your motor caravan and go to the reception office. Ask if you may use the site, explaining that you have a motor caravan.

45 These boards are at the entrance to a caravan park in Northumberland.

A.1 What is the name of the caravan park?

2 Is this site for both caravans and tents?

3 Is this park recommended by any particular group?

B. You arrive at the caravan park. You have not reserved a pitch in advance but think you would like to stay for three days. Ask at the reception if there is space, saying how long you wish to stay and how many people there are in your party. Remember, also, to give details of your car and caravan or tent, and to ask how much it will cost.

46 The Bell Hotel is on the main road in a small town.

A.1 Would you expect
   a) to stay the night here?
   b) to get something to eat if you were passing through?
   c) to be served with breakfast if you could stay the night?
   d) to get a five-course evening meal?
   e) to obtain something hot to drink while waiting for the next bus?

B. You are hitch-hiking with a friend in the North of England when you reach this town. There is no youth hostel. You go to the Bell to ask if you can stay there. What do you say?

47 This board stands outside a private house which, like many others in the area, caters for tourists.

A.1 What services are offered to the tourist?
   2 Could you get lunch here?
   3 Do you think you could buy wine or beer with your meal here? (*See* •48)

B. You go to Hillcrest to find rooms for two nights. You ring the doorbell and a woman answers. Ask her if she can offer you accommodation for you, your brother and your parents.

48 This sign is outside a small hotel in the Lake District.

• Alcoholic drinks may be served with meals only in hotels or restaurants which have the necessary licence.
• Some small hotels and guest houses serve meals and drinks only to people who are staying there.

• 'A.A.' stands for the Automobile Association, one of two large organizations which motorists can join; the other is the R.A.C.—the Royal Automobile Club. They offer many services, including advice about hotels and restaurants.

A.1 Does this hotel offer more than bed and breakfast?
  2 If you were staying here could you have a glass of beer or wine with your meal?
  3 What attraction is offered for the motorist?
  4 What attraction is offered for the casual passer-by?
  5 What do you understand by 'A.A. Listed'?
  6 If you arrived here on the day the photograph was taken, and had not booked a room, would you be able to stay here?
C.   You arrive at the Crow Park Hotel and ask at the reception desk if they have two rooms vacant for two nights. You want one room with a double bed and one room with two single beds. You would also like a shower in one room if possible. There are no rooms with a shower vacant, but there are rooms on the third floor at £6.50 each per night, breakfast included. You decide to take the rooms. Reconstruct the conversation with the receptionist.

49 You are staying in a hotel in a large city. This notice is at the reception desk.

A.1 Is a service charge added to these prices?
  2 Is the cost of breakfast included in the prices?
  3 Does your room have a television set?
  4 You and your cousin are staying here for two nights. You are sharing a room without private bath. You both have continental breakfasts. What is the total bill if V.A.T. is charged at 10%?
B.   You come to this hotel with your cousin and ask at the reception desk for a room for the two of you. You particularly want a room with a telephone. What do you say?

Tariff effective from May 1976

DAILY TERMS

Single Bedroom	£8.00
Single Bedroom with Bath	£9.50
Twin Bedroom	£11.50
Twin Bedroom with Bath	£14.00

Continental Breakfast extra 65p
Club Breakfast extra 90p
Full English Breakfast extra £1.25

SERVICE CHARGE

Service charges are included in all our Tariffs

VAT

VAT is an additional charge at the appropriate rate.

Thistle Hotels reserve the right to alter tariff charges without prior notification

ACCOMMODATION AND FACILITIES

105 Bedrooms, some with private bathroom, all with TV, radio and telephone.
Restaurant   All night porter

50 This board is on the corner of the Lake Hotel.

A.1 What do the initials 'R.A.C.' mean? (*See* •48.)

2 If you were not staying here could you have a meal at this hotel?

3 What does 'luncheon' mean?

B. You are planning your holiday and wish to stay for four nights in this town. Write a letter to the hotel: tell them when you would like to stay and ask them to book a room for you. Ask them, also, to tell you the price of the room when they accept your reservation.

51 This photograph shows some of the information in a leaflet about a large hotel.

A.1 In what *two* ways are charges reduced for a child of ten?

2 Can a child of two stay here free?

3 At what age must you pay the full cost of accommodation for a child? Is it 13, 14 or 15?

4 Are you allowed to bring your dog to this hotel?

C. You have a very large but very quiet dog. When you arrive at the hotel the receptionist says you cannot keep the dog with you. You say that the dog is used to hotels and to people, and insist that it is very gentle. The receptionist is afraid that the other guests will object. Reconstruct the conversation.

GENERAL INFORMATION

CHILDREN

ACCOMMODATION

Under the age of three, children are accommodated free.

Children under the age of fourteen sharing an adult's room are also accommodated free, subject to the availabi of suitable rooms are the time of booking.

This policy applies to one or two children sharing a twin room with two adults or a single room with one adu

FOOD

Childrens portions are available on request and will be charged at reduced rates.

DOGS

Whilst dogs are usually welcomed, the Hotel Manager do have the discretion regarding their acceptance.

SERVICE CHARGES AND VAT

Our tariffs include all services charges, VAT is an additio charge at the appropriate rate.

town

52 This sign in York marks the way into a very old street. Many of the street names in York end in '—gate'.

•'Footstreet' is an unusual word meaning a street for pedestrians only, now closed to vehicles.

- A.1 What is the name of this street?
- 2 Can you drive your car down this street?
- B. You want to get to the other end of Stonegate in your car. Ask a passer-by to direct you.

53 This new wooden building is near a main road in a city centre.

- A.1 Which street is this building in?
- 2 What is the purpose of the building?
- 3 Would *you* personally be able to use this building, or would you have to go elsewhere?
- 4 What is the meaning of the symbol near the entrance?
- B. You are in the city centre and your brother wants to go to the toilet. Ask a passer-by to direct you to the nearest men's toilet.

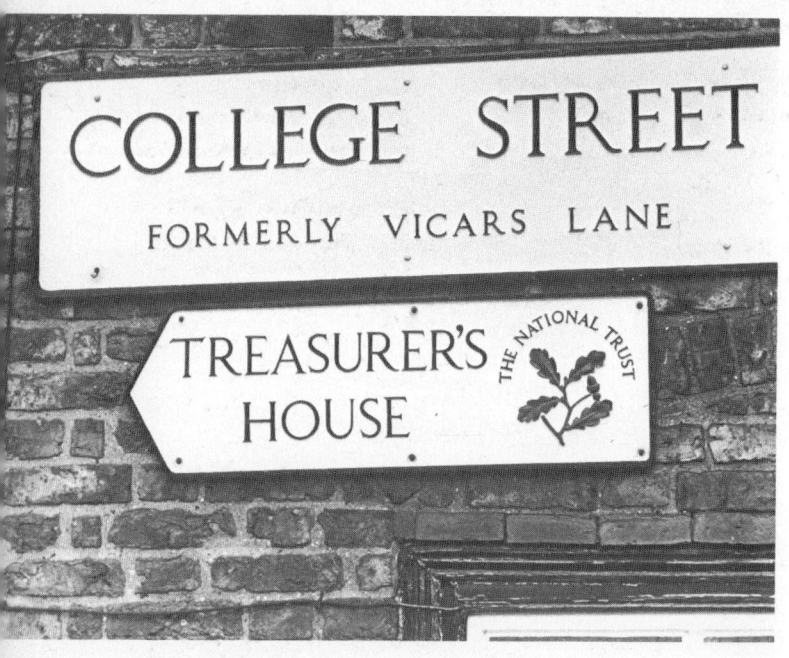

54 These signs are on the wall of a house in York.

• The National Trust for places of historic interest or natural beauty was founded in 1894 and is the largest private land-owner in Britain.

A.1 Is this house the Treasurer's House?

2 Who owns the Treasurer's House?

3 What is the name of the street in which you are standing as you look at these signs?

4 Has this street ever had another name?

B. You would like to see the Treasurer's House. Stop a passer-by and ask the way. Ask also if it is open to the public.

55 You see this sign as you are entering a small public garden.

A. Are you allowed to
a) walk on the grass?
b) play football?
c) eat your picnic?
d) play your guitar?
e) exercise your dog?
f) let the baby play on the grass?

B. You are doing one of the things which are *not* allowed, and an elderly lady tells you that you ought to go somewhere else. What do you say in reply?

56 This board is beside the entrance to a large building.

•Public libraries provide a free library service to the public. They lend books, supply information about local events and have copies of local and national newspapers and journals. You can borrow a book from the library only if you live in the area and have a library ticket.

•Shopping hours in England are generally between 9.00 a.m. and 5.30 p.m., but in some towns the shops close early on one weekday.

A.1 Why would *you* wish to visit this building
  a) To buy a book?
  b) To find out what events were taking place locally?
  c) To borrow a book?
  d) To read the local or national newspapers or periodicals?
  e) To buy some writing paper?
 2 When is early closing day in Gosforth?
 3 What do the abbreviations 'A.M.' and 'P.M.' mean?

B. You are staying for a few days in Gosforth and decide to go to the public library for information about places of interest in the area. What do you say to the assistant to explain what you want?

57 You are at a pedestrian crossing controlled by traffic lights. It is a very busy main road.

A.1 You wish to cross. What does the sign tell you to do?
 2 Where will you see the signal telling you that it is safe to cross?
 3 Should you cross when the 'walking man' signal is flashing?

B. You follow the instructions at the top, but nothing happens. Ask another pedestrian how to stop the traffic.

GOSFORTH PUBLIC LIBRARY	HOURS OF OPENING	
	MONDAY) TUESDAY)	9·00 A.M. – 8·00 P.M.
	WEDNESDAY –	9·00 A.M. – 1·00 P.M.
	THURSDAY) FRIDAY)	9·00 A.M. – 8·00 P.M.
	SATURDAY)	9·00 A.M. – 5·00 P.M.

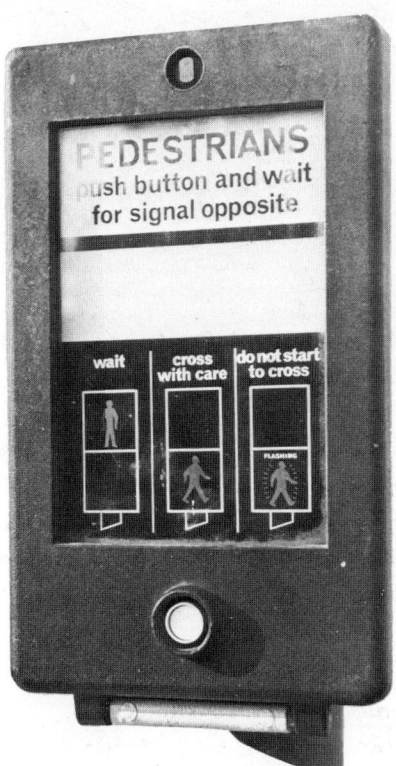

PEDESTRIANS push button and wait for signal opposite

wait | cross with care | do not start to cross

FLASHING

58 These signs are on a corner in a small town.

A.1 Which of the signs (top, centre or bottom) should you follow
   a) if you want to go to the lake?
   b) if you want a list of local caravan sites?
   c) if you want to camp for two nights?
   d) if you are looking for a good restaurant?
   e) if you want to know whether you can fish in the lake?

B. You have found the Tourist Information Office. What do you say if you are interested in one of the following activities: sailing, walking, angling, pony-trekking, painting, English literature?

59 These two notices are on a waste-paper bin in a main street.

A.1 What is 'litter'?
   2 What is the maximum punishment if you break the laws about litter?
   3 What does the sign tell you about the law concerning dogs?
   4 What is the punishment for breaking this law?

60 This notice is behind the glass door of a tourist information centre and provides information when the office is closed about services in the area.

A. 1 Where exactly would you go if you wanted to
a) buy some tablets for a headache?
b) report the loss of your passport?
c) buy a replacement fan-belt for your car?
d) have treatment for a bad wound?
e) obtain a meal at 2.30 on Sunday morning?

2 Why would you need a 'bureau de change'?

B. You have parked your car in the city centre, but when you return to the place your car has gone. You go to the police to make a report. What do you say to the policeman? Remember that you must give all the details about your car.

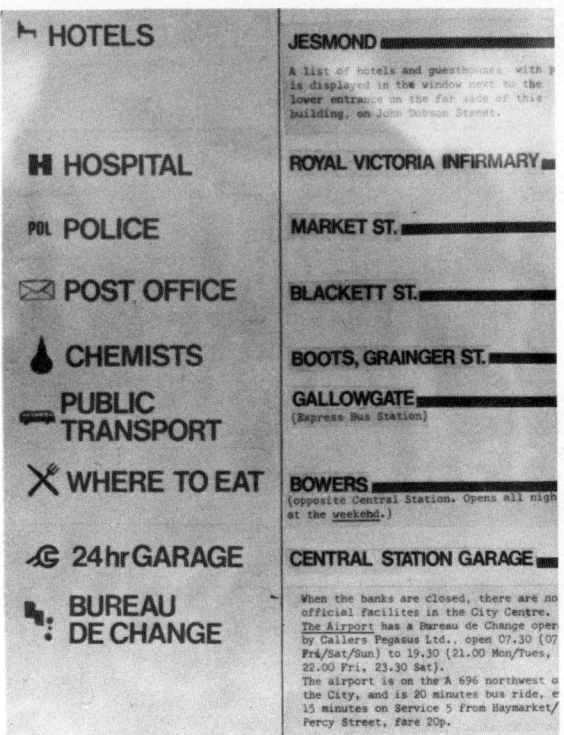

61 This board stands outside the Civic Centre. At this point you may go right or straight on.

A. 1 Should you go right or straight on
a) to inquire about work as an assistant teacher?
b) to register a death?
c) to tax a car?
d) to see a display of local artists' work?
e) to observe a council meeting as a member of the public?

C. Imagine that an English person has come to visit your home town and asks about places to see. You try to find out what the English person is interested in and to make suggestions. Reconstruct the conversation.

shops

62 This 'signpost' is in a small supermarket.

A.1 Which of the following items would you expect to see on the shelves in section 7:
   a) a loaf of bread?
   b) a tin of grapefruit juice?
   c) a bottle of wine?
   d) a jar of babyfood?
   e) a bottle of Coca-Cola?

63 This board shows the prices of eggs in a supermarket.

•Eggs are sold in half-dozens, but in this supermarket the word 'half' is covered by the price.

A.1 Three prices are shown. Why are they different?

2 Describe the eggs offered for sale. What three things, apart from the price, can you say about them?

3 How much do 12 standard eggs cost?

B. You take a box of eggs off the shelf and find that two of them are broken when you get to the checkout desk. What do you say to the assistant there?

64 This notice is on a checkout desk in a supermarket.

A.1 Is this notice
   a) an order?
   b) a polite request?
   c) a question?
   d) a suggestion?

2 You have put the goods you want to buy in a trolley. What does the sign tell you to do with them when you reach this point?

B. You have reached the checkout desk, but when you receive the total bill you find that you do not have enough money to pay for everything. What do you say to the assistant?

65 This board is on the railings in front of a building in a city street.

A.1 What service does this salon offer?

2 If you were in a wheelchair would you go here or to another salon offering the same service?

3 If you wished to phone to make an appointment what number would you have to ring?

4 Would this salon provide a service for *you* personally?

B. You enter this salon and take a seat. Explain exactly what it is that you want.

66 This board is on the pavement outside a shop selling Kodak films.

•Film sizes are expressed differently in English: 24×36mm. photographs are taken on 35mm. film, while 6×6cm. photos require 120 film. Your camera may use cartridges, cassettes or spools of film.

A.1 Which of the following would you expect to be able to buy here:
   a) a film for a cine camera?
   b) flash cubes?
   c) a film for 24×36mm. colour transparencies?
   d) a film for 6×6cm. black-and-white photographs?
   e) a cheap camera?
  2 What services are provided in addition to the sale of films?
B. You want a film for your own camera and enter this shop. Tell the assistant exactly what you want.

67 This notice is on the door of a tobacconist's shop that sells mainly sweets, chocolate and tobacco.

A.1 What else is on sale?
  2 Are the goods listed in the notice on sale at the normal price?
  3 What do all the abbreviations mean?
B. You have bought a packet of cigars costing 48p and you think that you were given the wrong change by the assistant. What do you say to check the price and the change?

68

These notices are inside a supermarket.

• 'McVitie's Rich Tea' is the brand name of a type of biscuit.

A.1 What is the price of one pound of flour?

2 If you have your dog with you when you come to this shop, what must you do?

3 Why are the same products sometimes sold at different prices?

B. You are shopping here and see the same jars of coffee on sale at different prices. You think there has been some mistake, and ask an assistant to tell you which is the correct price and

why two prices are shown. What do you say?

69

These posters advertise items for sale at reduced prices ('special offers') inside the shop.

A.1 What is offered other than food?

2 Explain the abbreviations: lb, pkt, oz.

3 What is the normal price of a tin of creamed rice milk pudding?

C. Imagine that you have been sent to this shop to buy a packet of breakfast cereal, a small jar of coffee, some cheese, two packets of biscuits and some frozen peas. You ask a shop assistant to help you and you tell her which

brands you require. You say that you only have a £5 note and she tells you how much change you will receive. Reconstruct the conversation.

70 This photograph shows one of the windows of a large store in a city centre.

- A.1 Why do you think people might be particularly interested in this window display?
  - 2 What exactly are you told about the prices of goods on display?
  - 3 At what time of year was this photograph taken?
- B. You would like to buy a small transistor radio which is strong enough to take camping. What do you say when you go into this shop? The normal price of the radio is £8.50. How much will it cost in the sale?

71 This sign is inside the entrance to a large city store. It is above the stairs which lead down to the lower sales floor.

- A.1 For which of the following would you go downstairs:
  - a) a boy's swimming costume?
  - b) trousers for a man?
  - c) an umbrella?
  - d) a pair of sandals?
  - e) a torch battery?
  - f) a snack?
  - g) a book?
  - h) a towel?
  - i) food for a picnic?
  - j) a pocket chess set?
- B. You are looking for a blue shirt in your size but cannot find any. Ask an assistant to help you.

country

72 This signpost is at Seathwaite in the Lake District.

- A.1 Could you drive a car along the route indicated by the signpost?
- 2 Where does this route lead to?
- 3 What other place would you pass on the way?
- B. You have gone for a walk while staying at the Borrowdale youth hostel and you are not sure which is the best way back. Ask another walker the way to the youth hostel.

73 This notice is attached to a gate on a Lakeland path.

•In Britain there are many public footpaths which go across private land. These paths are marked on large-scale maps of each area.

- A.1 What does 'Private Land' mean?
- 2 Do you think the walkers in the picture are allowed to use the path?
- 3 Are you allowed to take your dog this way?
- B. You are out walking and follow a track to a farm, but you are not sure whether or not you may cross the fields beyond. Ask the farmer's permission to cross his land.

43

74 This modern building is close to the main car park in Keswick.

•The mountain rescue services are free in Britain. They are normally contacted through the police. Emergency calls (for which you dial 999) are also free.

- A.1 What do the words 'Keep Clear' mean for the motorist and for the walker?
- 2 Why should you keep clear?
- 3 What kind of emergency would require the use of this building?
- B. You are walking on the fells when your friend falls and breaks a leg. You hurry down to the nearest telephone, dial 999 (the Emergency Calls number), and ask for the police. What do you say to the police officer who answers your call?

75 This notice is beside a public footpath which passes through fields close to a river. The word 'No' has been painted out by vandals.

- A.1 What are you not allowed to do in these fields?
- 2 What are you asked to do if you use this path?
- 3 You are looking for a place to have a picnic when you reach this notice. What should you do?
- B. You are walking along this path with a group of English friends. One of them throws down an empty drink can. What do you say to him or her?

76 This notice is beside a footpath near a farm in a Lakeland valley.

•Camping is restricted in England, especially in popular areas such as the Lake District.

A.1 Who owns this land?

2 If you could not camp here would you go further along the path towards the trees?

B. You are looking for a camp site away from crowds. Ask a farmer if you may camp somewhere on his land. You may have to convince him that you are trustworthy.

77 This board is beside a narrow country lane leading into a wood.

A.1 Who owns the wood?

2 Can you drive a car through the wood?

3 Do you have to have a permit to ride a horse in the wood?

B. You would like to visit the woods to see a fine waterfall there. Tell one of the foresters what you would like to see and ask him to direct you to the right place.

78 This plaque is fixed to a coin-box built into a pillar of stones. It stands in a popular area of the Lake District.

A.1 What kinds of land are owned by the National Trust (*see* •54) in the Lake District?

2 Are the Trust properties open to the public?

3 What does the Trust need money for?

4 How does the Trust obtain money?

5 What is the coin-box for?

79 This dummy is in a window in Keswick. It shows the inexperienced tourist the correct equipment for fell-walking in winter.

•**Fells are hills or mountains in the North of England and South of Scotland.**

A.1 What kind of trousers should you wear? Are jeans suitable?

2 What material should your shirt, stockings, and so on, be made of?

3 What kind of anorak is recommended?

4 What reason for wearing boots is suggested?

C. You do not have all the proper clothes to go walking on the hills, so you go to this shop and explain exactly what you require. You are asked for details such as size, colour, material and style. You think that the prices are too high but you decide to buy the articles. Reconstruct your conversation with the shop assistant.

places of interest

80 This board is outside the Tourist Information Centre in York.

A.1 What is the address of the centre?

2 Why would you visit the centre?

3 On which days of the week is this office open?

4 If you came to the office at 4.30 p.m. on a Saturday in March, would it be open?

B. Imagine that you have come to York and are interested in one of the following: steam locomotives, Yorkshire houses, castles, the Yorkshire countryside. Ask for the sort of information you might require.

81 You are visiting places of interest in Newcastle and have come to the entrance to the keep overlooking the River Tyne.

A.1 On which days is the keep open to visitors?

2 How much would it cost you and your family to go in?

3 Why is the town of Newcastle so called?

4 What does the abbreviation 'A.D.' mean?

5 What is a 'keep'?

TOURIST INFORMATION CENTRE

DE GREY ROOMS
EXHIBITION SQUARE · YORK

OPENING TIMES

JUNE TO SEPTEMBER Mon. to Sat. 0900 to 2000
                     Sunday   1400 to 1700

OCTOBER TO MAY Mon. to Sat. 0900 to 1700

TELEPHONE York 21756

DEPARTMENT OF TOURISM

ADMINISTRATIVE OFFICES

YORK⊙

THE KEEP
OF THE ROYAL CASTLE OF
NEWCASTLE UPON TYNE

BUILT BY KING HENRY II
A.D. 1172-1177 ON THE SITE
OF THE 'NEW CASTLE'
BUILT BY ROBERT, SON OF
WILLIAM THE CONQUEROR
A.D. 1080

OPEN TO THE PUBLIC EXCEPT ON SUNDAYS

ADMISSION 15p PER PERSON

CHILDREN (UNDER 12) 5p

82 The plaque is on a door at a small museum within the old town walls of Newcastle.

•Entrance to museums and art galleries was free in Britain until recently. You may now expect to pay a small charge at most of them.

A.1 Is the museum open
   a) at 1.00 p.m. on Saturday?
   b) at 9.30 a.m. on Wednesday?
   c) at 11.00 a.m. on Sunday?
   d) at 5.15 p.m. on Monday?
  2 How old is the original building?
  3 What was the building originally called?
  4 Do you go in by the door to which the plaque is fixed?
B. You go to the museum and find that it has just closed for the day. Ask the caretaker when it is open again, how much it costs to go in and where you can find out about its history.

JOHN GEORGE JOICEY MUSEUM
Old Holy Jesus Hospital c.1682

Open   Monday — Saturday incl.
10 a.m   UNTIL   6 p.m
Admission   FREE

Entrance this door

83 This stone is over the doorway of a small house near Newcastle.

A.1 Why is George Stephenson famous?
  2 How long did he live here?
  3 What important event took place here in 1814?
  4 What was 'Blucher'?
B. You see this house and read the words on the stone above the doorway. You would like to see the inside of the house so you knock on the door to ask if you may do so. What do you say to the person who opens the door?

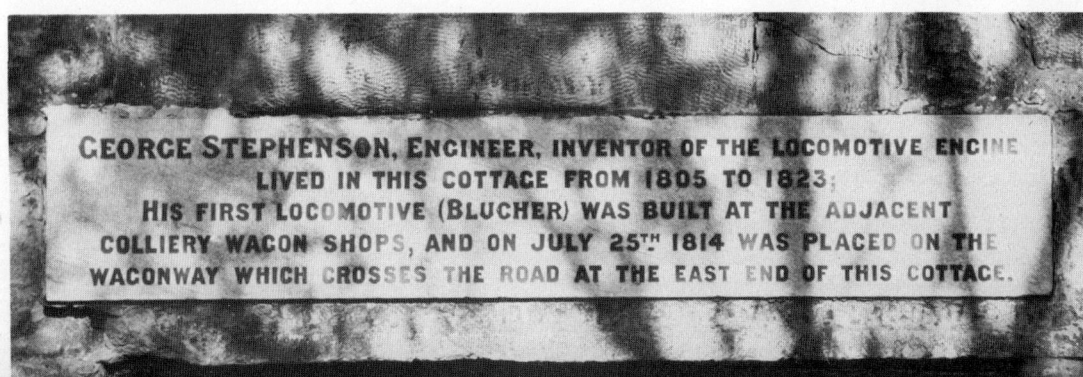

GEORGE STEPHENSON, ENGINEER, INVENTOR OF THE LOCOMOTIVE ENGINE LIVED IN THIS COTTAGE FROM 1805 TO 1823; HIS FIRST LOCOMOTIVE (BLUCHER) WAS BUILT AT THE ADJACENT COLLIERY WAGON SHOPS, AND ON JULY 25TH 1814 WAS PLACED ON THE WAGONWAY WHICH CROSSES THE ROAD AT THE EAST END OF THIS COTTAGE.

ROMAN FORTRESS

This plaque marks the site of the Porta Principalis Dextra or North Western Gate of the Roman Fortress of which the foundations as rebuilt circa A.D.300 lie just below ground.

84 This plaque is fixed to part of the town wall in York.

A.1 What can you learn about the early history of York from this plaque?

2 Can you still see the Roman fortress here?

3 What does 'circa' mean? It is often abbreviated to 'c.' as in photograph 82.

B. You would like to see some of the Roman antiquities in York. Ask at the Tourist Information Centre for information about what there is to see, where to see it and how to get there.

85 You see this board at the top of the cliffs at Tynemouth and decide to visit the ruins of the priory and castle.

A.1 Where can you park your car?

2 How much does it cost to park?

3 Who can enter for half-price?

4 How much would it cost *your* family to visit the castle and priory?

C. You are visiting Tynemouth with an English friend and you go to the castle and priory. You ask why the priory is inside the castle. Your friend thinks that the castle was built to protect the priory from Viking raids, but you think it was built in the best place to guard the entrance to the river. Reconstruct the conversation.

TYNEMOUTH PRIORY AND CASTLE ENTRANCE
← **Car park inside Castle.**
ADULTS·**10p.** CHILDREN (under 16 yrs.) & O.A.P's·**5p.**
CARS·**5p.** MOTOR CYCLES·**2½p.**

86 You are interested in historic buildings and have come to this one in the centre of York.

    A.1 In what century was the Kings Manor built?

    2 Which English kings stayed here?

    3 Who was Francis Place and when did he live in the Kings Manor?

87 You are walking along a lane in the country when you see a number of tall stones standing in a field. You go into the field.

    A.1 How much does it cost to visit the stone circle?

    2 How old is it thought to be?

    3 What are visitors warned not to do?

    4 What was the stone circle thought to have been used for when it was built?

    B. Imagine that you have visited this stone circle. Try to describe it to an English friend, using the details given on this plaque.

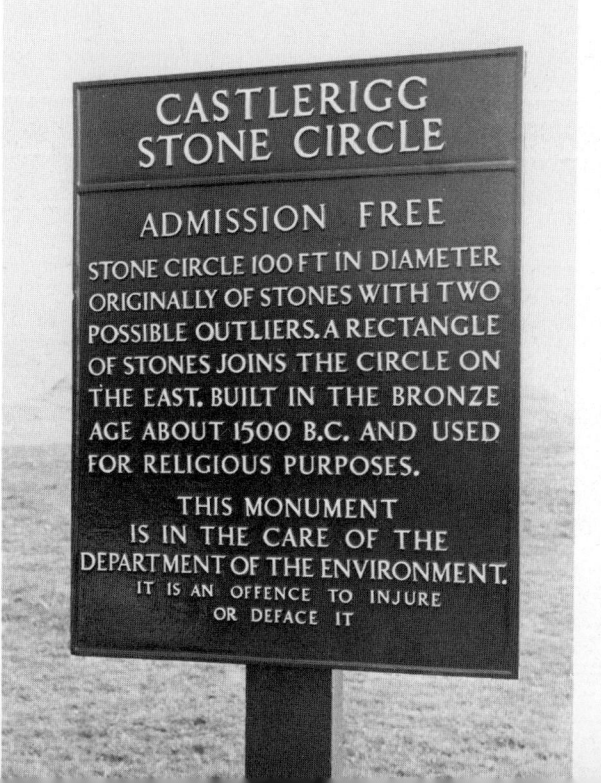

seaside

88 You are walking along the promenade in a seaside town when you see these two clocks.

A.1 What do the clocks tell you?

  2 When would you go swimming while the tide was high in the evening?

  3 At what times could you fish from the rails of the promenade at high tide?

  4 At what time could you explore sea caves at the foot of a cliff?

89 You are at a small harbour and see this notice near the steps going down to the water.

A.1 You see that there is a red flag at the top of the pole which has this notice on it. Would you

  a) go for a swim?

  b) go fishing here?

  c) play on the sand?

  d) go on the sea in a small boat?

B. You are hoping to go for a swim in the sea, but it seems rather rough. Ask a local fisherman if it is safe.

90 This photograph shows the back of a seaside oyster bar.

A.1 Are oysters the only fish on sale here?

2 What is the name of the owner of the oyster bar?

3 For what is the bar noted, according to the sign?

B. You would like to try some shell fish and decide to buy some shrimps and mussels for yourself and your two friends. What do you say to the person serving?

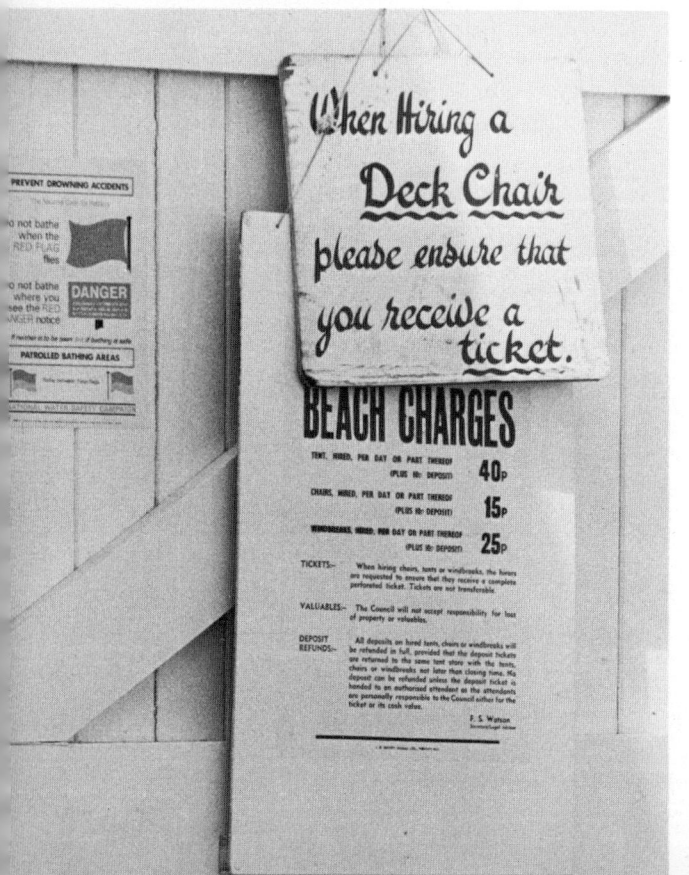

91 This notice is on the door of a shed where deck-chairs, beach tents and windbreaks may be hired.

A.1 When you hire a deck-chair what should you receive in addition to the chair?

C. You hire a deck-chair but lose the ticket. When you return the chair you explain what has happened and ask the attendant for the 25p deposit which you had to leave with him. The attendant refuses to return your deposit so you say that you will not return the chair. In the end, you receive your 25p. Reconstruct the conversation.

92 You see this poster as you are walking along the promenade and decide that you would like to visit Marineland.

A.1 What is the main attraction at Marineland?

  2 What other animals can you see at Marineland?

  3 Where in Morecambe is it situated?

  4 It is 9 o'clock in the morning. Is Marineland open?

B. You are trying to decide where to spend an hour or two. Your English friend would like to go to a railway museum but you would like to go to Marineland. Tell him, or her, why you think Marineland is better.

93 This is the entrance to a pier.

•A toffee apple is an apple coated with toffee and sold on a stick like a lollipop.

•Candy floss is sugar thread, spun into a loose, fluffy mass, also sold on a stick.

•A number of seaside resorts have, or used to have, long piers or jetties built out over the sea. Holiday-makers walk along the piers and enjoy the amusements which are usually found on them. Many piers are now being demolished as they are too expensive to repair.

A.1 What popular game is offered here?

  2 What snacks containing meat are available?

  3 What sweets are on sale?

B. You decide to buy something to eat. What do you ask for? Make sure you know exactly what you are buying.

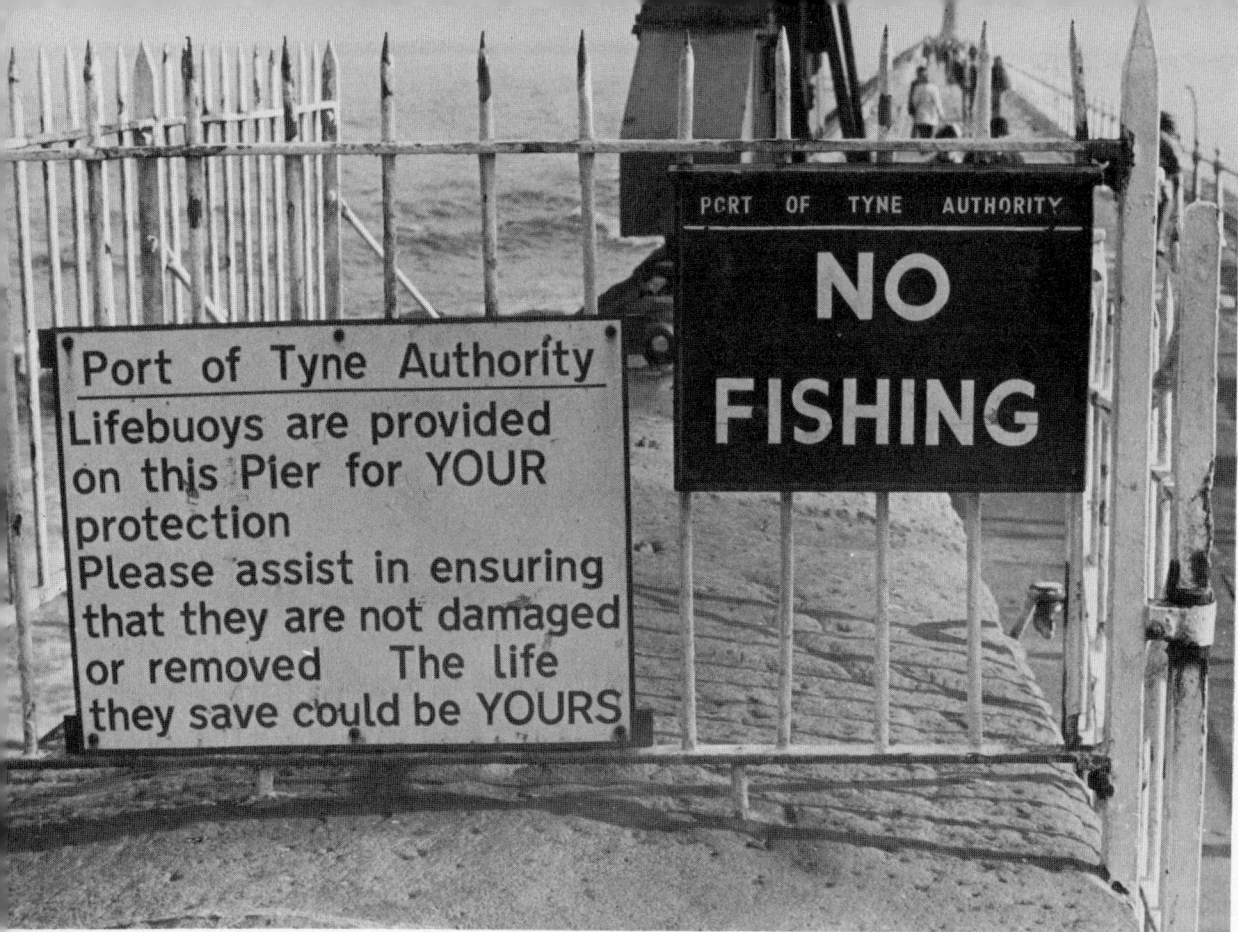

94 You see these notices as you walk on to the North Pier at the mouth of the River Tyne.

A.1 Why are lifebuoys provided?
  2 What is everyone asked to do?
  3 What are you not allowed to do here?
  4 Who is in charge of the pier?
B. You are a keen fisherman and have borrowed what you need to go fishing at the seaside. You do not know if it is best to fish from the beach, the rocks or the pier. Ask another fisherman for advice about each place.

communications

95 You are looking for a post box and find this one.

A.1 When will your letter be collected if you post it
 a) at 5.30 p.m. on Saturday?
 b) at 8.00 a.m. on Thursday?
 c) at 10.00 a.m. on 24th December?
 d) at 4.15 p.m. on Saturday?

2 When is there no collection?

B. You have missed the collection from this box, and decide to go to the nearest post office. Ask someone to direct you.

96 You have found the post office. This notice gives information about hours of business and of services.

A.1 Is the post office open if you arrive
 a) at 4.30 p.m. on Wednesday?
 b) at 2.30 p.m. on Saturday?
 c) at 10.00 a.m. on Sunday?
 d) at 9.30 a.m. on Tuesday?

2 When and how can you send a telegram if the post office is closed?

3 By what time must you post a letter here if you want it to be delivered in Gosforth by the first delivery next day?

B. You want to send a telegram and the post office is open. Ask the person behind the counter how to send one and how much it will cost.

192. SAVILLE ROW

Collections

Monday to Friday	Saturday
1 8.30AM	8.30AM
2 NOON	NOON
3 2.PM	
4 4.PM	
5 5.45PM	

Sunday	NONE
Good Friday	3.30PM
Public Holidays	NONE
Christmas Day and Boxing Day	NO COLLECTION

GOSFORTH
BRANCH POST OFFICE
NEWCASTLE UPON TYNE.
NE3 1AA

HOURS OF BUSINESS

WEEKDAYS	SUNDAYS, GOOD FRIDAY BANK HOLIDAYS & CHRISTMAS DAY
9. 0 a.m. TO 5. 30 p.m. 9. 0 " TO 1. 0 " (SAT.)	CLOSED

TELEGRAMS May be dictated from a kiosk at any time.

PUBLIC TELEPHONES The nearest kiosk is outside this office.

DELIVERIES

	TIME OF DELIVERY	LATEST TIMES OF POSTING AT THIS OFFICE TO CONNECT
LETTERS	7. 0 a.m.	7. 30 p.m.
	11. 0 " (Not Sat.) NE3 only	10. 30 a.m. (Not Sat.)
PARCELS	8. 45 a.m.	

TERATIONS
COLLECTIONS

97 At the post office you ask about the cost of sending a letter to your home town. You are given this leaflet.

A.1 How much does it cost to send a 50 gram letter to a European country?

2 Is there an extra charge for letters sent to Malta?

3 What is the cost of sending a postcard?

4 Do small packets automatically go by airmail?

B. You would like to send a book home as a present but it would cost too much to send by air. Ask how much it would cost by surface mail, and how long it would take.

Air Mail Europe
Air Mail labels are not necessary

Letters & Postcards
are sent by air whenever this will result in earlier delivery.

Letters Not over	20g	50g	100g	250g	500g	1kg	2kg
	10p	18p	24p	48p	92p	160p	260p

The letter rates to Gibraltar, Malta and Cyprus are the same as to the rest of Europe.

Postcards	7p

Printed Papers & Small Packets
will go by air only if sent as Letter packets and prepaid at the full Letter rate, shown above.

Newspapers
registered at the Post Office will be sent by air under the same conditions if prepaid at the following 'All-up' newspaper rates:

Not over	20g	50g	100g	250g	500g	1kg	2kg
	6p	9p	14p	18p	32p	60p	110p

98 You are staying with a friend in London and wish to arrange to visit another family. Here are the costs of telephone calls.
• STD (subscriber trunk dialling) means that you can make long-distance calls simply by dialling a series of numbers, rather than going through the operator.

A.1 The second family also lives in London and you can dial the number directly. How long can you speak for 3p

a) at 9.00 p.m. on Friday?

b) at 10.00 a.m. on Monday?

c) at 4.00 p.m. on Tuesday?

2 If the second family lived 80 kilometres from London how much would it cost for a 6 minute call at the same times?

Inland Telephone Calls

From telephones without a coinbox

	Dialled		
	Peak rate Mon-Fri 9am-1pm	**Standard rate** Mon-Fri 8am-9am 1pm-6pm	**Cheap r** At all oth times
	time for 3p	time for 3p	time for 3
Local			
STD Lines	2 mins	3 mins	8 mins
Non-STD Lines	3p untimed	3p untimed	3p untim
Trunk			
Up to 56 km	30 secs	45 secs	3 mins
Over 56 km	10 secs	15 secs	1 min
To Channel Islands	10 secs	10 secs	24 secs
To Irish Republic	8 secs	8 secs	15 secs

99 These are examples of charges for calls to Europe.

•International telephone calls may be made by ISD without going through the operator if you live in certain countries. To make a call to a country outside Britain dial
1. the international code—010
2. the country code—33 (France), 49 (Germany), 46 (Sweden)
3. the area code—78 (Lyon), 221 (Köln), 40 (Malmö)
4. the person's individual number—say, 456399
For example: a friend in Lyon—010 33 78 45.63.99.

A.1 Is it more or less expensive to make a call through the operator?
  2 How much would it cost to make an ISD call lasting two minutes from England to your home on a Sunday?
  3 Do these charges also apply to calls made from a public telephone like that in No. 100?
B. You are unable to dial direct to your home. Ring the operator and ask for the call that you want.

International Telephone Calls

Examples of some of the new charges
From telephones without a coinbox

	Dialled		Connected by operator for any reason
	Standard rate Mon-Fri 6am-8pm	Cheap rate At all other times	
	time for 3p	time for 3p	charge for 3 min
Charge Band 1 Belgium France Netherlands	7.20 secs	9.60 secs	£1.11
Charge Band 2 Germany (FR) Italy Spain Sweden Switzerland	5.14 secs	8.00 secs	£1.41
Charge Band 3 Greece	4.00 secs	6.00 secs	£1.71

100 If you make a call from a public telephone box the instructions may look like this.

•'Pips' are very short, high sounds all on the same note.
•Emergency calls (dial 999) are free. When the operator answers you should state the service you require and give your name. You may contact the police, fire brigade and ambulance service in this way.

A.1 What coins do you need to pay for the call?
  2 How do you find out how much money to have ready?
  3 When do you put the first coin in?
  4 When must you put more money in?
  5 If you have had a car accident what number must you dial to call an ambulance?
C. You do not know the number of a friend whom you wish to telephone. You ring Directory Enquiries. The operator asks for the town, the name, the initials and the address of your friend. Here they are: H.R. Purvis, 23 Front Street, Nantwich. The number is 0270 23791. 0270 is the STD code for the town. (If you were in the same town you would dial only 23791.) The operator does not hear your friend's name correctly and you have to spell it out. Reconstruct the conversation.

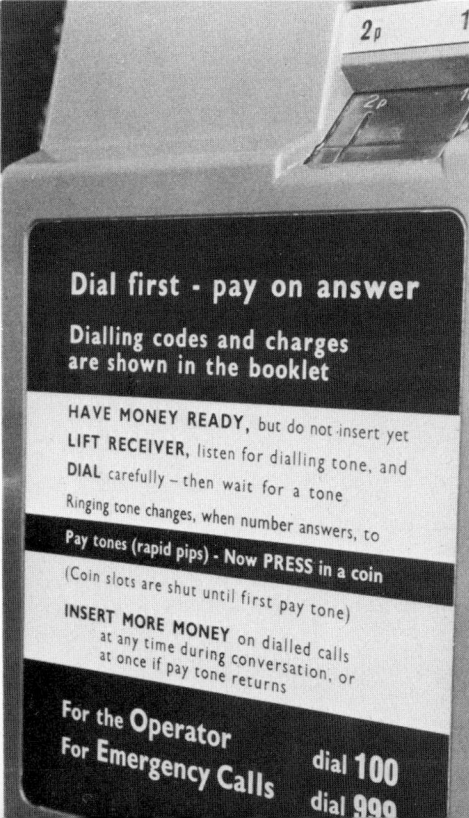

Dial first - pay on answer

Dialling codes and charges are shown in the booklet

HAVE MONEY READY, but do not insert yet
LIFT RECEIVER, listen for dialling tone, and
DIAL carefully – then wait for a tone
Ringing tone changes, when number answers, to
Pay tones (rapid pips) - Now PRESS in a coin
(Coin slots are shut until first pay tone)
INSERT MORE MONEY on dialled calls at any time during conversation, or at once if pay tone returns

For the Operator   dial **100**
For Emergency Calls   dial **999**

leisure

101 You are walking past a concert hall and see this board outside.

•'O.A.P. s' stands for old age pensioners (*see* •16); that is, women over 60 and men over 65 who receive a state pension.

A.1 Does the board refer to a past, present or future event?

2 Does the concert take place in the afternoon or evening?

3 Who can pay less than the full price to go in?

4 Can you find the spelling mistake?

B. You are interested in going to this concert, but you are not quite sure what kind of band is playing. What might you ask in order to find out?

102 You notice this board at the top of a street leading down to the river in York.

A.1 What sort of leisure activity is advertised?

2 How much would it cost for *your* family?

3 Where do the cruises go?

4 What does 'Circumstances permitting' mean?

B. You think you might enjoy a cruise, but would like some more information because you are nervous of boats. What questions might you ask?

103 You are walking along a road near Newcastle on 10th April when you come across this board at the entrance to a park.

A.1 What three sports take place here?

2 When can you see horse racing here?

3 Why might you go to Brandling House?

B. You would like to go to watch some horse racing. Ask a passer-by when and where the nearest races are, and what time they start.

HIGH GOSFORTH PARK

NEWCASTLE RACES

NEXT MEETING | **17·19· APRIL** | FIRST RACE | SAT. 1·30 P.M. | MON. 2·00 P.M.

NORTH EAST EXHIBITION CENTRE

JOHN JACOBS GOLF CENTRE

BRANDLING HOUSE BANQUETING ROOMS

BORDER MINSTREL HOTEL

S° SQUASH NEWCASTLE

104 This poster is outside the ground of Newcastle United Football Club, and shows details of two matches.

• 'Res.' is short for 'Reserves'.

A.1 Where is Wednesday's match being played?

2 At what time does the match on Saturday start?

3 Would you see the same Newcastle team on both Saturday and Wednesday?

B. Your English friend wants you to come with him to watch a football match. You are not very keen. Ask who is playing, when and where the match is and how much it will cost to get there and to go in.

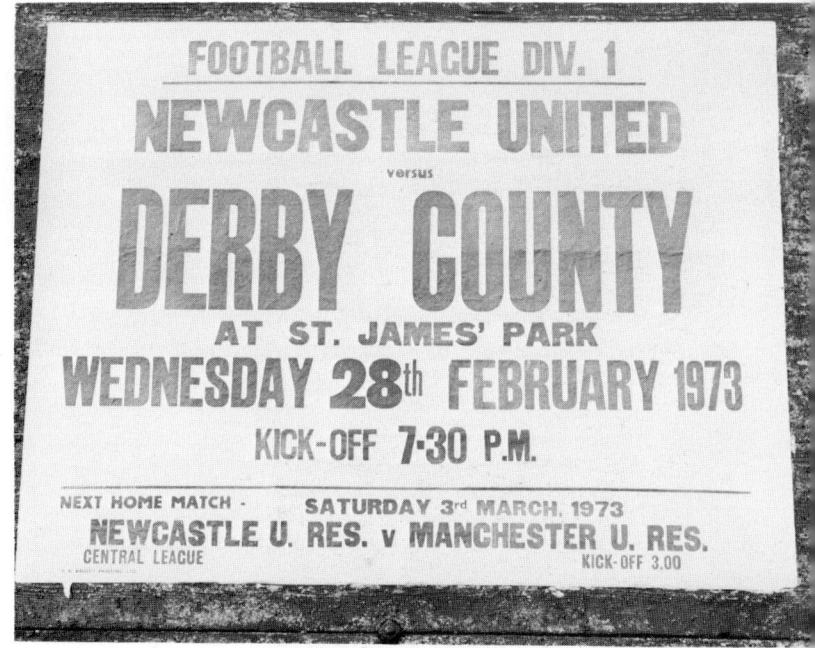

FOOTBALL LEAGUE DIV. 1

NEWCASTLE UNITED

versus

DERBY COUNTY

AT ST. JAMES' PARK

WEDNESDAY 28th FEBRUARY 1973

KICK-OFF 7·30 P.M.

NEXT HOME MATCH - SATURDAY 3rd MARCH. 1973
NEWCASTLE U. RES. v MANCHESTER U. RES.
CENTRAL LEAGUE   KICK-OFF 3.00

105

You see this board outside some shops in a small seaside town.

• It is necessary to be a member in order to get into many night clubs and similar places of entertainment.

A.1 What three kinds of entertainment are offered?

2 Is the entertainment offered to all members of the public?

3 If you went to the Inn on the Bay often, would you always see the same entertainers?

B. You would like to take your English hosts out for an evening. Suggest that you go to the Inn on the Bay and say why you think it would be enjoyable.

106

You are passing the Winter Gardens theatre when you notice this window.

A.1 What is this office for?

2 Where can you buy a theatre ticket?

B. You wish to book seats for the theatre. Ask for two seats in the circle for a performance by the Royal Ballet, including the date and the time of the performance.

107 These posters are outside the People's Theatre.

A.1 When could you see *Shrivings*?

  2 What would you expect to see and hear if you went to listen to the Robles Trio?

  3 If you wish to go with a friend, which is the best day to go to this theatre?

B. You have bought two tickets for the theatre but find that you cannot go. You take the tickets back to the box-office and ask for your money back. What do you say?

108 You are going into a cinema when you see these notices at the entrance.

A.1 You are 13 years old.

   a) Are you allowed to see an AA film?

   b) When can you get in for half price?

   c) Can you go by yourself to see an A film?

  2 You are 15 years old.

   a) Which types of film are you allowed to see?

   b) Can you get in for half price?

   c) Can you go by yourself to see an AA film?

  3 Who can go to see an X film?

C. Imagine that you are queuing behind two 15 year old teenagers who are trying to buy seats in the stalls at a cinema showing an X film. The cashier questions them about their age. They persuade her that they are over 18 and are allowed in. Reconstruct their conversation.

danger

109 You see this sign where a new road is being constructed.

A.1 What kind of danger is there here?

2 Does the danger exist for
a) drivers of cars?
b) cyclists?
c) drivers of heavy lorries?
d) pedestrians?

110 You are walking up a country lane when you see this sign.

A.1 Are you allowed to go beyond this sign?

2 What does the sign tell you about the land beyond it?

3 What might happen to you if you ignored this sign?

C. You are walking through some fields in the country when you are stopped by an angry man carrying a gun. He says that you are trespassing. You tell him that you are not English and you do not understand what he means. He explains and you apologize. Reconstruct the conversation.

62

111 You are travelling by car along an open road when you pass this sign.

A.1 What should the driver now look out for?

2 Is it certain that you are now in danger?

3 Does the sign tell you how to avoid the danger?

B. As you pass the sign you see that the driver (an English person) did not notice it. What do you say?

112 You are in a car following this tanker along a main road.

A.1 What must you remember if you want to overtake this tanker?

2 What does this tanker contain? Why is it dangerous?

B. This tanker is involved in an accident and overturns: the contents spill out on to the road. Go to a telephone, dial 999, and ask for the police. Tell them what has happened and why it is particularly dangerous.

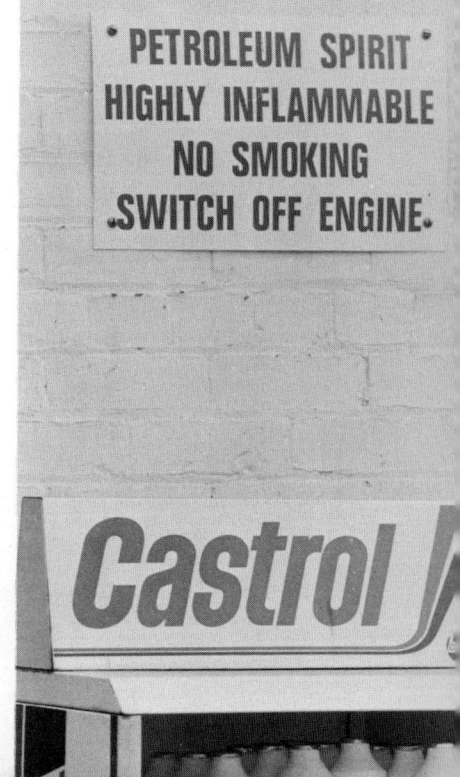

A 686 to Penrith
Via Hartside Summit
Altitude 1900 ft.

WINTER CONDITIONS CAN BE DANGEROUS

113 This sign warns about dangers which may be met on the A 686 road. The road is sometimes closed.

A.1 What dangers are likely?

  2 When would they be met?

  3 What is the main reason for the existence of these dangers?

B. You are hitch-hiking and have been given a ride in a car on this road. The conditions look dangerous. What might you say to the driver?

114 This sign can be seen at all garages where petrol is on sale.

A.1 If you stop for petrol what two things must you remember to do?

  2 Why should you do these two things?

B. You stop at this garage and your English friend, who has not seen this sign, brings out a packet of cigarettes. What do you say?

PETROLEUM SPIRIT
HIGHLY INFLAMMABLE
NO SMOKING
SWITCH OFF ENGINE

Castrol

FORESTRY COMMISSION
TAKE CARE
DO NOT START
FIRE

115 You are out for a walk in the country when you see this sign at the side of the road leading to a wood.

A.1 What does the sign warn you not to do?

2 Why is the danger so great here?

3 What ought you to do to avoid causing the danger?

B. You have heard on the radio that the danger of fire is very great at this place. You think that perhaps you should not go into the wood. Ask the advice of a forester, explaining why you are worried.

LIFEBUOY

In an emergency
Throw lifebuoy beyond victim
Draw into victim's grasp
Pull victim slowly to safety

Don't delay - seconds count

Do not interfere with this
lifebuoy or rope.
A life may depend on it

GLASDON
LIFEBUOY
STAND

Designed &
manufactured by
Glasdon
Limited
117-123 Talbot Road
Blackpool FY1 3QY
Lancs. Tel 22076-9

116 You see this advice printed in large letters on a red box beside the sea.

A.1 When would you use a lifebuoy?

2 Describe in your own words how you would use a lifebuoy.

3 What are people asked not to do in order to make sure that the lifebuoy is always ready for use? Why?

C. You and your friend decide to go for a swim in the sea. Just as you are about to enter the water a lifeguard stops you. He explains that the sea is dangerous, but you reply that you are very good swimmers and it is very hot weather. The lifeguard is angry that you do not take any notice. You promise not to go swimming here, but ask about a swimming pool. Construct this imaginary conversation.

medical

117 You are taking someone to hospital to receive emergency treatment after a camping accident. You reach this gate.

•Medical attention in Britain is normally free, but a small charge is made by the chemist for each prescription made up, unless the medicine is for a child or an old person.

A.1 What is the name of this hospital?

2 Is this the right entrance for you?

3 Your friend has been kept in hospital and you wish to visit him or her. Is this the right way in?

B. Your friend has been burned in an accident with a cooking stove. You both go to the accident department of the hospital. Explain what happened, and give the name, age, address and telephone number of your friend.

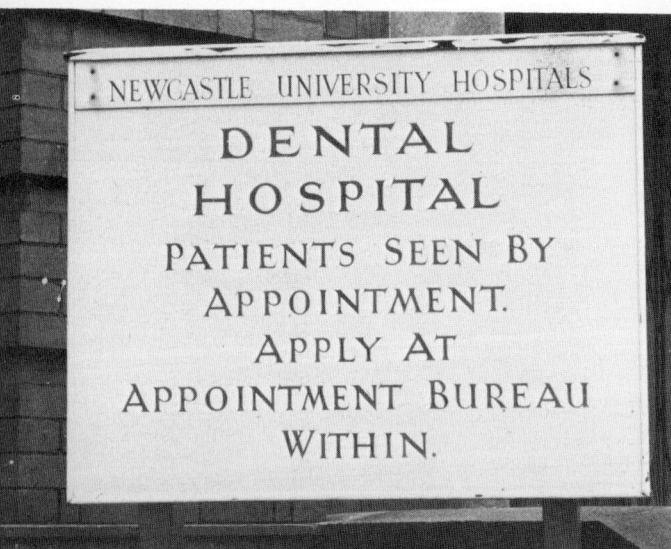

118 This board is at the entrance to a large building in the city.

A.1 What is the name of this building?

2 What kind of treatment can you get here?

3 What should you do to arrange treatment?

B. You have bad toothache and come to this hospital hoping to get immediate treatment. Go to the office and explain the situation. Ask if they can see you straight away.

ORIGINAL FLAVOUR

'Milk of Magnesia' REGD.

For stomach upsets indigestion and constipation

Shake well before using

 *Chas. H. Phillips*

119 This is the label from a bottle which can be bought in many chemists' shops.
- 'Milk of Magnesia' is a brand name.

A.1 Would you take this mixture
- a) if you had a headache?
- b) if you had a stomach ache?
- c) if you had a cough?
- d) if you had a sore throat?

2 What must you remember to do before taking the medicine?

B You have a very bad headache and go to the chemist's to buy some pills. You ask the chemist's advice. What do you say?

COLD AND INFLUENZA MIXTURE

Helps to relieve symptoms in Colds and Influenza

DOSE

Adults and children over 12 years, 10ml (two teaspoonfuls). Children 5 to 12 years, 5 ml (one teaspoonful).

The dose should be taken every two hours.

Not recommended for children under 5 years.

KEEP ALL MEDICINES OUT OF THE REACH OF CHILDREN.

Camphor 0·15%; Ether Spirit 0·62%; Squill Vinegar 3·5%; Strong Ammonium Acetate Solution 1·6%; Benzoic Acid 0·2%. Anise Oil 0·03%. Rectified Spirit 5·6%.

120 You and your family have caught bad colds. This is the label on a bottle of medicine you have bought (*see* •117).

A.1 How should you measure the amount to take?

2 How often should you take the medicine?

3 What is the correct dose for a person
- a) 3 years old?   c) 15 years old?
- b) 8 years old?   d) 20 years old?

4 What does the label warn you to do?

C. You have been feeling unwell for a few days, with headaches and sickness. You go to the doctor, who asks you about your symptoms, what you have been doing and what you have been eating and drinking. He gives you a prescription and advises you to consult your own doctor when you return home. Reconstruct the conversation.